–273.15

Work by Peter Reading

Collected Poems: 1: POEMS 1970-1984 (Bloodaxe Books, 1995)
Water and Waste (1970), *For the Municipality's Elderly* (1974),
The Prison Cell & Barrel Mystery (1976), *Nothing For Anyone* (1977),
Fiction (1979), *Tom o' Bedlam's Beauties* (1981), *Diplopic* (1983),
5x5x5x5x5 (1983), *C* (1984)

Collected Poems: 2: POEMS 1985-1996 (Bloodaxe Books, 1996)
Ukulele Music (1985), *Going On* (1985), *Stet* (1986),
Final Demands (1988), *Perduta Gente* (1989), *Shitheads* (1989),
Evagatory (1992), *Last Poems* (1994), *Eschatological* (1996)

Collected Poems: 3: POEMS 1997-2003 (Bloodaxe Books, 2003)
Work in Regress (1997), *Ob.* (1999), *Marfan* (2000),
[untitled] (2001), *Faunal* (2002), *Civil* (2002)
𝄞 (2003)

-273.15 (Bloodaxe Books, 2005)

RECORDINGS

The Poetry Quartets: 3 (Bloodaxe Books/British Council, 1998)
[with James Fenton, Tony Harrison & Ken Smith: 30 mins each]
The Life Works of Peter Reading (Lannan Foundation, 2003)
[22 DVD videos: total length 22 hours: *see* www.lannan.org]

ON READING

Isabel Martin: *Reading Peter Reading* (Bloodaxe Books, 2000)

PETER -273.15
READING

BLOODAXE BOOKS

ISBN: 1 85224 679 0 paperback edition
      1 85224 724 X limited hardback edition of
                    200 signed and numbered copies

First published 2005 by
Bloodaxe Books Ltd,
Highgreen,
Tarset,
Northumberland NE48 1RP.

www.bloodaxebooks.com
For further information about Bloodaxe titles
please visit our website or write to
the above address for a catalogue.

Bloodaxe Books Ltd acknowledges
the financial assistance of
Arts Council England, North East.

Cover printing by J. Thomson Colour Printers Ltd, Glasgow.

Printed in Great Britain by
Bell & Bain Limited, Glasgow, Scotland.

To Patrick Lannan

ACKNOWLEDGEMENTS

Some of these pieces were commissioned and broadcast by BBC Radio 3. Other material was first published by Cleveland State University Program in Linguistics, www. qualm.co.uk, and *The Times Literary Supplement.*

The author acknowledges the financial support of the Lannan Foundation.

*(After the heatwaves: Heat Death, Entropy,
Absolute Zero...)*

Noye, Noye,
Could you handle,
Atop t'others,
337 species of *Pheidole*
New to Science
And recently charted
By Edward O. Wilson?

*

'Chuck 'em aboard;
Chuck 'em aboard me bucko mate
An' let's heave aweigh.'

and didya read how a survey of all them Brit birds and butterflies shows there's some sorta population decline?, [Yes, in a series of censuses that combed about every square yard of England, Scotland and Wales over forty years, more than 20,000 volunteers managed to count each bird, native plant and butterfly they could find. They reported that the populations of all the species surveyed were in sharp decline – many extirpated completely.] and didya read how two surveys of 1,200 sumthin plants showed a decrease of 28%? [Yes, frail planet undergoing its sixth great extinction – Cambrian, Devonian, Permian, Triassic, Cretaceous, Holocene   ]

Ahoy! Noye! *Oimoi!*
32% of world's amphibian species,
Brink of extinction.
And what of the fissipeds,
Having toes that are separated
From one another, as dogs, cats, bears,
And similar carnivores?
What of the fissirostrals?
Of the Elegant Trogons?
The Meerkats?

UK numbers of summer-visiting *Cuculus canorus*
Down 50% in 30 years –
Scientists at the Rothamstead Research Centre
Say that seven or eight species
Of moth caterpillars, important in the bird's diet,
Are in serious decline:
Caterpillars of the Tiger Moth,
The Magpie Moth,
The Lackey Moth,
The Figure-of-eight Moth
(The larvae over-winter,
And this recent warm, wet
January and February weather
Favours fungal pathogens
Which kill them)…

*

'F'c's'le, standing-room only.
Y'all look lively *Now!*'

For I will consider my cat Tikka:
For she is an atheist;
For she does the eight rolly-polly in the mornings;
For this is the manner in which she *chooooses*
To express her gratitude and affection;
For she will leap upon the volumes
Heaped upon me by the *TLS* for review
And knock them all asunder
(This being an empirical demonstration
Of anarchy, and, to mention Lucretius,
Tantum religio potuit suadere malorum);
For she doth remark that 'In Egypt we was *Sacred* and all that';
For she doth consider how God is defunct;
For she can can-can, mew and chew biscuits and consider
How she and I and my wife are also defunct.

*

'OK, chuck 'er aboard,
And yous get down the gangplank too –
Next port o'call's Ararat,
(Can't see as we'll make it, mind,
Bad bearings, too much of a maelstrom,
D'ye see?, d'ye see?, d'ye see?)'

*

For she hateth the notion of God, prefering physics.

Trebinje; six a.m.;
autumn; bank of the river,
a burgeoning *Ficus*; pausing
to pick one, I flushed from wet roots
a Little Bittern (tiny,
fast-flying, wing coverts cream
against black – and I'd heard it barking
and barking through the night
every two or three seconds).

Outside the Café Dalmacia,
opposite, there was a young girl
sweeping; I crossed a bridge
and asked for *pivo* – she brought it,
along with a local newspaper –
that was a good place, good beer...

Thence to (*then* peaceful) Dubrovnik.

My father gave me a copy
Of *Living Things for Lively Youngsters*
When I was six.
It explained, *inter alia*,
The differences between
Frog, toad and newt spawn
(All nearly extirpated, now).

*

'Slop a few dollops in the bilges, then, Shipmate.'

*

Thanks, Noye.

thus we know that Global Warming, rather than causing gradual, centuries-spanning change, will push the climate to tip-point, fast. The ocean/atmosphere system controlling their frail planet's climate will change things radically – maybe in less than a decade. [The struggle naught availeth.] And consider the geopolitical implications. And consider the urgency of underwhelmed societies, the haves and have nots. And consider the 4% of the Arctic ice cap melted per decade since about 1970, the decline of the North Atlantic's salinity reduced over the past forty years, the possible effect of this on the Great Atlantic Current, the cooling of much of Europe and the U.S. if the flow ceased, the droughts, the dust-bowls and the ashes... [You, at the back, should've sat up and fuckingwell paid attention   ]

Sir, Sir, will eu emploie
Cockes, kytes, croes,
Rookes, ravens, divers hoopoes,
Cuckoes, curlues, kakapos,
Ich one in his kinde?

*

'Ham, Ham, it's muckle late:

Nothing can ever be done,
Things are intractably thus,
Those having precognition suffer
Heat Death beforehand.'

*

Noye, Noye,
I see Mi people in deede and thoughte
Are sette full fowle in synne.
Bestes and fugols with thee thu may take,
He and shee, mate to mate;
Nathless, hit be Mi lykinge
Eall lif for to destroye –
Destroyed eall thes weorold shall be,
E'en eower shippe, gentil Noye,
Eower cargo's rich biodiversitye,
Each cell sincan.

*

'I dree mi Weird,
Wi due regard to eower deityship.'

and didya read how them corporates own all the water?,
sure gonna trigger big global shit in a few years,
[Nights, the cops' 'copters are beaming the NO-GOs;
days, the CCTV yellow/blue/white vans
circuit the zones most likely to get hit.]

and didya read how them albatrosses in the Antarctic
is gettin extinct through gettin all snagged in them
two-mile fish-lines?,
[These are the days of the auspices' headlines;
days to consider the vast ineluctable,
vast ineluctable.]

Gavin Buchanan Ewart,
alive and kicking in Putney
and eulogising Wystan
and quaffing yeast Young's in the Duke's...

[Dreams are perfidies.]

and didya read how them rain forests is burnin 6,000 acres an hour – that's 1.6 acres per second, Jeez! [The school mag. *Juvenilis* piece, 'Bonfire', a puerile Keatsesque thing, proved microcosmic after all: *Chill was the eve and no breeze blew, And through faint haze a red sun set On spiders' webs bedecked with dew. He contemplated, as he stood, The embers, failing, fall to ash, Last sighs expiring from once sap-green wood.*]

For it is My Likinge
Mankinde for to anoye.

*

Sir, here are Lions, Leopards,
Birches, Hawthorns, Rosebay Willowherbs,
Horses, Oxen, Peccaries,
Shrews, Voles, various species of Ants,
Goats and Sheep,
A duo of *Alligator mississippiensis*,
A couple of Nine-banded Armadillos,
Two *Lycosa tarentula*,
Don't forget the Pygmy Nuthatches,
(Too late for the Ivory-billed Woodpeckers,
But chuck in a pair of Pileateds),
Coyotes, Chamois, Chimps,
Woodlice, Carp, Morons,
Budgies, Yosemite Bears,
Rats, Pipistrelles, Sprats, Brats,
Yeasts, Yobs, Silver-back Gorillas,
And here are Doves, Ducks, Drakes, Redshanks,
Kyrie eleison, diverse Bacteria,
Don't forget the Slime Moulds...

*

Clang, clang, clang: All aboard for Ararat.

*

Oi!, never omit the Natterjack Toads, the Palmate Newts,
The Slow Worms, the Gnats, the Gnus, the Tape-Worms, the

First light at the Stubblefield Pool
solo and hoping for plump Tench,
and, by the time of first darkness,
three were hooked, landed and gently
slithered again to their own depths.

By Dawes to the Marl Pond at dawn,
tackle prepared against sunrise.
As light issued and the split-cane
was neatly secured in its notch,
out of the blue a Kingfisher
landed and perched for ten seconds
on the Greenheart tip of the rod.
There was epiphany, surely;
and there followed, lured by fat worms
(fetched out of the lawn in the dark),
four bright Rudd, bronze-girthed and red-finned.

And therefore this celebration
of formative, insular days,
in inadequate threes and eights.

CLIMATE COL...

...to see why we're ...
...gun has ...once interested in ab... of cli
mate ch...

There the ... in getting ser
ous. ...but it a ...back again, a
te ...ay in temperature ...eratures en
...ded in ...ty of ...rise ... The
...ta show ...temperate dramatic shifts
in avera... ...ure took place in the past with sh...
spec. ...in some ...t just a ...ears.

The case for an was hurt... by a theory regarded as the
...t likely explan... for the a... ic changes. The eastern U.S
a northern Europ... ...t seems, are warmed by a huge Atlantic
O... in current that ...s north from the tropics—it a's why
B...in, at Latitude's ...ude, is relati ly temperate. Pumping
...u warm, moist air, this ...eat conveyor current gets cooler, and
...ser as it moves north ...hat causes the cu... nt to sink in th
N...rth Atlantic, where it heads south again in t... ...cean d... s
sinking process ...ws more water from the s... ...upe in
the roughly circular cu... nt on the go.

But when t ...limat warms, according to ... ...eory, fresh
water from me Arctic glaciers flows inv... ...North Atla ic
lowering the c ...t's sal ity—and it ...y and tendency to
sink. A warme nate alt increase ...nfall and runoff into
the current, further lowering its saltiness. As a result, the con-
vey r loses its main motive force and can rapidly collapse
turning off the huge heat pump and altering the climate o...

much of the Northern ...

Scientists aren't sure what ...
warming that triggered such ...happens in
the remote past. (Heat, it wasn't ...
h ir factories.) But th... ...lat... tion ...

An... ...and e...er sour... deg...d tro...
atmo... ...ic that ...ther ...ok Earth
collap... wer... ...avingly similar to to ...
As the ...n... gan drawing to a close
for ev... ...e ...eratures i ...reeply t...
rose to levels nea... ...d to... ...es. The ...e ab... y
plunged as the c... ...way ...p... ...ntly sh down ...efore ...o the
"Younger Dr... periods... ...20-year ...ice age con
ditions as abyss is an Abru... ...ge th... ...ished in Europe
at t... ...me.

Though Mother Nature... ...e s... e... ...ate change
the one that may be shaping... ...e, ...e ...ience te...
...t us. In 2001 an intern... ...p... o... Climate exper... on
clut... ...that there is increa... ...gly ...g ...ence that most of the
...al warming observed ...er the pas... ...years is attributable to
...uman activities—mai... the burning of fossil fuel... ...ch as oil
and coal, which release ...at-trapping ca... bon dioxide. Indicators
of the warming include shrinking Arcti... ice, melting alpine glac
ies, and markedly ...arlier springs at m... ...ny lo... ...ct ...s. A few
...rs ago such ch... n es seemed signi ...ant to ...k... for our
kids or grandkids. T day they seem p... cus of a car... n, that
may not conveniently wait until we're ...tory.

Newly discovered fossil evidence indicates that more than 100 million years ago in (what is now) China, an adult female Psittacosaurus was buried in a mudslide, apparently attempting to protect its 34 nestlings. This aggregation suggests, to palaeontologists from the Dalian Natural History Museum in China and Montana State University in Bozeman, that certain of the *Deinosauria* behaved rather more like birds than like today's lizards, 'caring for' their young, even after the eggs had been laid, incubated and hatched...

*

'Belay, lubber! That's one Helluva long line ya got there!
Well, well, well; let that be a lesson to y'all –
Pipe all hands, Mr Boatswain. Stand by to cast off, pronto.'

nk that major climate nset of an ice age, took rs to unfold. Now they know ansitions can occur in less The probable trigger of abrupt ges, at least i the Northern e, is the shutdown of a huge ocean he Atlantic Ocean. The cur is dense, salty water that flows north e tropics and sinks in the North At h water is pumped into the h can occur. from b Atlantic. if fres northerly part of the current – will, as global warming melts Arctic ice – its salin drops, making it less dense. This diminishing density can prevent the wate sinking in the North Atlantic, stopping the current's flow. Much of Europe and the U.S. could become colder and drier if that happened, cientists hav decteted disquieting trends: 3% to 4% of the Arctic ice cap melted per dec Arctic's largest ice shelf broke up near Ellesmere Isla releas an ice-dam, freshwater lake into the ocea (scientists believ that the similar melting, 8,200 years ago triggered an episode of abrupt climate change The North At has decline continuously for the past 40 years – the most dramatic oceanic change ever measured. The flow of cold, dense water through a North Atlant channel near Norway – part of the Great Ocean Current that warms northern, urope – has dropped by at least 20% since 1950, suggesting that the curren is weakening. Many researchers now believe the salient question not 'could it happen?', but

Noye, Noye,
Do you have space
For circa one million
Mexican Free-tailed Bats,
Tadaria brasiliensis (mexicana),
Out of the roosting slots
Under Congress Avenue Bridge, Austin, Texas?
Also a brace of stray Aardvarks (*Orycteropus afer*)?

*

'Chuck 'em aboard, Messmate.'

*

Thanks, Noye.

and didya read how we fished them sand eels
    out of existence?,
sure gonna fuck them kittiwakes good, plus
    fulmars and puffins,
no goddam plankton, ya know?, for them mother
    sand eels to feed on,
due to that global shit, ya know?, heatwave
    followed by deepfreeze?,

A field-note remarks clemencies:
firmament, cerulean;
Mount Pinos, 9,000 feet;
at the summit, Clark's Nutcracker
(chunky grey body, black wings,
white secondaries, white outers,
black central rectrices);
creak of packed snow underfoot;
Jeffrey Pines' fumous vanilla;
Steller's Jay; Pygmy Nuthatch;
White-headed Woodpecker...

                                   Suddenly,
evening; descent into shadow
of the deep valley ahead –
its dark vermicular flume.

Oi!, Oi!,
I got a ruck of Echidnas 'ere
(They stink like shit,
But they gotta place,
Just same as you'n me);
Also a bunch of Amsterdam Albatrosses,
Blue Petrels,
Black-faced Sheathbills,
King Penguins,
Northern Rockhopper Penguins,
Salvin's Prions,
Eaton's Fulmar Prions,
Kerguelen Petrels,
Kerguelen Shags [*Phalacrocorax verrucosus*],
Black-bellied Storm Petrels,
Indian Yellow-nosed Albatrosses
[Note the wholly white heads
Characterising them from the Atlantic morphs],
Indian White-chinned Petrels,
White-headed Petrels,
Suffercloses, Shriekspowers,
PseudododoDantos, AnonyMoses,
Messrs Billing & Coo,
Noye's Larks, good as *mooo*…

*

'Yeah, yeah, yeah;
Clang, clang, clang!
All aboard for Ara, Rat.'

climate collaps accordingly, the spotlight in search is shifting from gradua change. In 2002 the National A Sciences issued a report concl human activiti could trigge change. Last year the World Ecc run in Davos, Switzerland, incl sion at which Woods Hole Oceanographi tution in Massachuetts, urged makers t consider the implicat change within two decades. Scientists used to thi chan like the o thousands of yea such dramatic to than a decade climate chan Hemi current in t driven by Meanwhile, in North America, drought coupled with hig winds could ravage the Midwest's farmlands, past conveyor shutdowns are link to massive fires in North America, which left telltale ash in Arctic ice. Fr deprived the flow of warmth from the tropics, northern Europe would become m like Labrador – or Siberia. Though triggered by warming, such change would p ly cause cooling in the Northern Hemisphere, leading arsher winters in much, U.S. and Europe, d cause massive droughts, turning farmland d forests to ash icture last fall's Calif s a regular thing. Or imagine similar dis ng nuclea powers such as Pakistan or lobal warming may be bad news for future generati that the Pentagon's strategic planners are grappling with it. The threat has riveted attention on this: Global warming, rather than causing gradual, cent anning change, may be pushing the climate to a tipping-point. ing evidence s the ocean-atmosphere system that controls the world's climate can lurch from one state to another in less than a decade – cientists don't know how close, system is to a critical threshold. But abrupt climate change may well occur, not too distant future, need to rapidly adapt may overwhelm many societies – thereby upsetting the geopolitical balance of po if abrupt nate change is on the way, the driving force will be the current known as the Great Conveyor w sweeps north through the Atlantic, carrying warmth from the tropics to the e trn U.S. and northern Europe before looping south. If the current shuts down – which apparen can occur rapi during times of global warmin the huge heat p goes off, potentially causing drastic weather changes in just

After three years in orbit,
into the Utah Desert
(neither parachute functioning),
data capture – a billion,
billion atoms and ions
from our modest sun.

The objectives of Genesis,
to peer at the very beginnings
of our little solar system
six billion years ego [sic].
But scientists have been left
peering into a large hole.

(Not for the first time,
Genesis goes all to shit.)

meanwhile, in the region of the constellation of Fornax, below Orion, here is the image of a composite set of 800 exposures, taken over the course of 400 Hubble orbits over eleven days. Many of the stars in the image are some 76, 254, 048, 000, 000, 000, 000, 000 miles from Earth, their light generated more than 13 billion years ago, and having taken that long to reach Hubble. [The light from Mars, which is presently more than 125 million miles from this frail planet, takes ten minutes to reach us. The Big Bang seems to have been approximately 14 billion years ago.]

'And *this* one is taken from the Mosque, darling; it took *ages*, though, to get there. And *these* are the Smiths – I can't remember *where* they are from.'

Ubi sunt:
Mr Boote
Who taught us English,
Had an ebony walking-stick
With a silver top
(We fantasised his having been
A war-hero shot down in his Spitfire –
Hence the limp);
Mr Bottomly,
Taught us French (or tried);
'Dicky' Bird,
Fondler of bums as we attempted to read Shakespeare;
Mr Hollowood,
Fine teacher of Chemistry
(Only one eye –
An accident in the lab.)…

*

'No space, matey,
For the deceased;
Get over the gunwale yerself,
Or else stay there and drown
(Only the Great Algonquian Mugwump
Could tell us how many cubits up
The waters will prevail *this* time).'

CLIMATE COLLA

An old pattern
reemerge—warfare
defining human life.

is happening

something drastic

little doubt that

"By 2020 there's

EVIDENCE OF SCARY CHANGE

The climate
could change
radically, and
fast. That would
be the mother
of all national
security issues.

Ahoy!
I have here
Various selachian fishes
(Including Hammerheads),
Together with diverse cetaceans…

       *

'Piss off;
We got more than enough, more than enough.'

Past midnight, and my umpteenth Zinfandel.
I type the Science Spotlight for tomorrow's
edition of the *Global Sentinel*:
  The earth is losing species at a rate
  comparable with the mass extinctions of
  the Cambrian, Devonian, Permian,
  Triassic and Cretaceous. The Golden Toad
  lived on a mountain ridge in Costa Rica,
  and has not been seen there for 15 years.
  The Hawaiian Thrush was extirpated by
  destruction of its forest habitat,
  pathogens brought by introduced mosquitoes,
  and competition from non-native species.
  The Hawaiian Crow is also now extinct.
  Pantanodon madagascariensis
  (a fish from Malagasy) disappeared
  when swamps it lived in were converted to
  fields to grow rice. A 'new' Brazilian
  amphibian has not been sighted since
  it was discovered 80 years ago.
  What's happening now is more than can be seen
  anywhere in the fossil record. These
  annihilations, taking place for reasons
  of climate change and new disease emergence,
  are indications of climacteric things
  which will affect us and our fraily balanced
  productive economic systems, *soon*.
In my same column thirty-eight years back:
  The earth is threatened by its own pollution...
  Western Industrial Man is facing, *now*,
  not just a challenge but a climacteric...
(Those in the front seats should have paid attention.)

For I will consider our shippe's cat.
For having performed the rolly-polly and curly-paw,
For entertainment she tackles the tenfold cogitations.
For first she frets over rainforest depletions.
For secondly she condems our otiose CO_2 emissions
For these fuck up her atmosphericals.
For thirdly she bids a peremptory adieu to biodiversicals.
For fourthly she regrets that 8 Burmese Pythons,
4 Emus, an Anaconda and 12 Colombian Red-tail Boas
Have been left back at the zoo awaiting *Diluvium*.
For fifthly she grieves the accelerating pace
Of melting Antarctic glaciers
(Smokestack and tailpipe gas)
For these drain the West Antarctic Ice Sheet –
Region containing enough ice
To raise sea levels 20 feet
(Tough luck, Bangladesh, New Orleans).
For sixthly she calculates the numbers
Of *Cuculus canorus* visiting UK
Down 50% in 30 years.
For seventhly she flinches
From the cathode-ray tube's dire tidings.
For eighthly she strenuously denies deities.
For ninthly their accipitrine unleashing scares her shitless.
For tenthly she apprehends devenustation.

Before-dawn-dark. Above the sibilant creek
and the great Pacific's distant tumble and swash:
poor will; poor will; poor will; poor will; ip –
a four-flush of weak iambs, and that was that.

and didya read how that
Everest snow-line's
five miles above where it
was fifty years back?,
and didya read how them
climate extremes is
happenin faster and
faster and faster?,
and didya read how that
Everest snow-melt
(climatic change again,
see what I mean like?)
fills all them lakes in the
Himalayas?, –
when them lakes *burst*, better
look out *then* mate!,
and didya read how (and
this sounds crazy)
this Global Warming'll
cause a Great Ice Age?,
and didya and did

Me boots an' clothes are all in pawn,
Hruh!,
Go down, ye blood-red roses, go down,
An' it's flamin' draughty roun' the Cape o' Storm,
Hruh!,
Go down, ye blood-red roses, go down…

Cap'n Noye!, Cap'n Noye!,
Belay!
Now, afore we man the capstan bars
For to heave the lead,
Take a look at these little critters
As 'll occypy no room,
No room at all –
The *rickettsiae*,
Parasitic microorganisms
Intermediate in structure between bacteria and viruses
That live in the tissues of ticks
And other arthropods
And cause disease when transmitted to man.

*

'A pox on all an' sundry!
We got vermin a-plenty below decks!'

*

OK!, OK!, OK!,
Keep yer wool on, Noye!

Well, my ol' mother she said to me,
Hruh!,
Go down, ye blood-red roses, go down,

Me darlin' son, come home from sea,
Hruh!…

Now,
As for the North Atlantic Eel
(Down 99% in twenty years –
Global Warming adversely affecting breeding routines?,
Overfishing?)…

*

'Nope!'

*

Tham Liverpool gals don't have no combs,
Hruh!,
Go down, ye blood-red roses, go down…

Now,
Howsabout this bit of brand twig,
All that's left of the Amazonian rainforest
Systematically razed
By Brazilian slave-labour
To produce charcoal
For USA pig-iron manufacture?

*

'Too fucking late!'

*

They comb their hair with kippers' backbones,
Hruh!…

Now,
Here's a choice item!,
Here *is* a choice specimen!
This here li'l' lady
Stands just 95 cm high,
Lived in a goddam *cave* for chrissake!,
H. floresiensis,
Any chance, Noye?

*

'A gradely gal, no doubt,
(Victim of the heatwave?)
But there's nothin' to 'er,
'Er's a bony li'l' packet an' no mistake!
'Tis too late, me buckeroo,
'Er's too tardy for *this* catastrophism.
Let's 'ave just one small taraxacum,
Then we'll scatter some spume.'

*

Go down, ye blood-red roses, go down.

Who'd've ever thought
that the bozo who came to *lunch*
would've *stayed*?!

[Well, we won't live long, we know *that*;
but, while we do, let's love, thus.]

2x
Alpine Chough,
Cheetah,
Chihuahua,
Chub,
Chiffchaff,
Plain Chachalaca.

＊

'Now, Mr Bosun,
Let's get the Hell outa this dock.'

Field note : Veracruz ; torrential rain ;
Johnston and I in a dengue-infected village ;
dumped truck-tyre-reservoirs of ~~breeding~~ mosquitoes ;
Snail Kites (2 juvs. ~~male~~ one female) ;
9 Yellow-headed Vultures ,. ↵↵ (*Cathartes burrovianus*)
slouched in unilluminated shacks,
those who have yielded to
the unequal struggle.

\#   l.l. 10

indent
& increasingly
diminutive {

dengue-infected microcosm
3 kites
9 vultures
~~of m~~
those/who are yielding to
the unequal struggle
torrential rain
torrential rain
torrential rain

\#   l.l.10

~~273.15~~
~~\# l.l.10~~
Kelvin   Stet ✓